More than meets the eye

A plain guide to Christianity

More than meets the eye

A plain guide to Christianity

Steve Chalke

Hodder & Stoughton
LONDON SYDNEY AUCKLAND

British Library Cataloguing in Publication Data
A record for this book is available from the British Library.

ISBN 0 340 64190 8

Designed and typeset by Typograph, Irby, Wirral, Cheshire.
Printed and bound in Great Britain by Cox & Wyman Ltd, Reading, Berkshire

Hodder and Stoughton
A division of Hodder Headline PLC
338 Euston Road, London NW1 3BH

Contents

Introduction

BORING, irrelevant, or just good for a laugh – what do you make of Christianity? Thousands of people simply dismiss it as a hangover from the past or a convenient crutch for the emotionally vulnerable and intellectually deficient. But are they right? I think not. I'm increasingly convinced that what Jesus taught makes sense, and that Christianity is as exciting, relevant and practical today as it's ever been. So don't be too hasty to write it off – there's more to it than meets the eye.

And like Christianity, there is more to this book than meets the eye. It would have been impossible to write without the help of my wife, Cornelia, and all of my friends and colleagues at the Oasis Trust. In particular: Simon Parish, Charlotte Mungeam, Lyn Ransom and Paul Hansford, who have laboured with me for many hours to produce a book we hope you will find both informative and fun.

Steve Chalke

Part One

There Has to be More

1

Wake me when it's over

EVERYWHERE I go, people tell me the same thing: church is boring. And I have to admit, they have a point. Being a vicar, I go to a lot of churches, and many of them are extremely dull. Many church services are so boring that God is probably asleep as well. Listening to a sermon can be slightly less interesting than watching gloss paint dry. One church I came across had a huge notice board outside which said: 'Why face depression alone? Come to church'.

For weddings and a funeral

We all have images in our minds about what church is like. We've seen it on television or at weddings. The crusty vicar in flowing clerical robes singing hymns that should have died with their composers. Or the minister swamped at the front of the church by a huge pulpit and dressed in black, looking just like Darth Vader.

I once heard a story about a new British ambassador to

Austria, attending his first official function. Overcome by the emotion of the event, a lavish banquet, he turned to the woman next to him and asked her to dance. She was decked in jewels and wearing a beautiful red dress. She turned him down flat. 'For one thing,' she said, 'this is a banquet, not a ball. You don't dance at a banquet. For another thing, the orchestra are playing the Austrian national anthem. And for a third, I am the Cardinal Archbishop of Vienna.'

Pillows out!

It's common knowledge that sermons are really a chance to catch up on your sleep. When I was younger, I used to get so bored and sleepy during sermons that I would get double vision. To my horror, there would be two preachers talking merrily away at the front of the church! I used to count the ceiling tiles, the organ tubes, the number of pages in the hymn book: anything to pass the time.

According to a recent poll, if all the people who fell asleep during sermons were placed in a row, end to end on the floor . . . they'd all be a lot more comfortable than they are sitting in their pews!

In some cases, it almost seems as though the preacher is catching up on sleep too, even though he may be talking at the time! There's even been a book written to provide help for those who can't sleep, called *101 Things To Do During A Dull Sermon!*

A young priest, just out of the vicar factory, was preaching for the first time in front of his new congregation. He was very nervous, and as he read out his carefully prepared sermon, he could feel himself shaking. At the end of the service, an old man came up to him and offered some 'constructive criticism'. 'There were three things wrong with your sermon, young man,' he said. 'Firstly, you read it. Secondly, you read it . . . badly. And thirdly, it wasn't worth reading in the first place!'

Nothing to make a song and dance about!

In the film *Sister Act*, nightclub singer Whoopi Goldberg hides out from the mob in a convent. Bored by the convent life, she is given the task of whipping the choir into shape. It needs it: the poor nuns are to singing what Henry Cooper is to flower arranging! The kind of music she chooses brings the nuns back to life and packs the church. But, complains the Mother Superior, it is definitely not suitable for church.

'This is not a theatre or a casino!'

'Yeah, but that's your problem, see,' replies Whoopi Goldberg. 'People like going to theatres and they like going to casinos, but they don't like going to church. Why? Because it's a drag!'

Let's face it, if church were a West End show, it would close after a week. The critics would slam it, and the financial backers would pull out. Yet people have been going to church for nearly two thousand years. Why? If it really is so boring, why on earth *do* people go there, week after week, sometimes for their entire lives? Don't they know any better? Have they simply got stuck in a rut? Do they need more company than they get from the post office or in the supermarket queues? Is it possible that for some reason they actually *like* singing 300-year-old hymns?

Or do they, perhaps, know something that the rest of us don't?

It's not what you do, it's the way that you do it

The truth is that whilst some churches are exactly like the stereotype we've been describing, there are many more that aren't. A church, you see, is only as boring or exciting as the people in it.

One of my favourite jokes concerns a young man woken abruptly by his mother, very early on a Sunday morning.

'Get up!' she says. 'You've got to go to church!'

'I'm not going!' the son replies. 'I don't want to go.'

'You have to go,' the mother says, sternly.

'Why?'

'Two reasons. One, because it's Sunday and we always go to church on Sunday. And two, because you're the vicar!'

There is, in fact, far more to church and Christianity than just what you see on a Sunday morning, or on *Songs of Praise*: far more than meets the eye.

2

Big cats and tasty snacks

BUT WHAT? After all, Christianity is a quaint hangover from a bygone age. Christianity, just like many church buildings, seems like a relic of the Victorian era. If we're honest, most of us think of Christians as a bunch of harmless, anorak-wearing train-spotters. Or worse! We suspect they're a bit weak in the head. Christianity provides them with the insulation they need against the harsh realities of life. We think of Christians as being like the animals in Noah's Ark, escaping from the flood. Except that there's no flood.

Not that big a deal

It's not that people are strongly opposed to Christianity. Few of us would want to feed all Christians to the lions, like the Roman Emperor Nero. It's just not that big a deal. In fact, it's really quite difficult for us to understand *why* Nero ever wanted to make pet snacks of such a dull group of people as the Christians.

Most people don't think that Christianity is evil. They just think that it has little or nothing to do with real life. It's just a crutch for the mentally or emotionally vulnerable to lean on.

Yet Nero *did* feed Christians to wild animals. He ordered them to be flayed alive, crucified, exiled, decapitated, speared, hacked, forced to work the mines, tortured, set alight, torn limb from limb, and subjected to a whole host of other unhappy endings. All for public enjoyment and the price of admission.

Never a dull moment

And the amazing thing is that Christians made no secret of their 'subversive' faith. In fact, they actively told other people what they believed, even when it meant certain death. What's more, they frequently expected the people they told about their faith to become Christians themselves, knowing that they too would end up on the barbecue.

Being a Christian in the early days of the Church was anything but dull. It used to be said that it was generally 'exciting, challenging and short'! Either the early Christians were very stupid indeed, or there was something so valuable about the Christian faith that thousands upon thousands of people were prepared to die for it. Because the persecution of Christians didn't stop with Nero; it continued on and off for another 250 years.

In the first few centuries AD, Christians considered their faith to be so relevant to their lives that they were prepared to die for it. And quite a few people who weren't Christians were prepared to kill Christians for it. Some Emperors were fanatical about getting rid of Christianity. They called Christians 'atheists', because they didn't believe that the Emperor was a god. And they were so afraid that these 'atheists' could destabilise the Empire that they strung them up in huge numbers.

Praise God and pass the ammunition

This hardly sounds like the Church we know. Can you imagine anyone believing that Christians were a threat to peace and security? I mean, *Thought for the Day* is hardly a hotbed of revolution. The blue-rinse-and-zimmer-frame-brigade don't exactly look set to take over the world! In fact, Christianity looks about as exciting as a hot mug of Horlicks! Somewhere along the line, surely, someone must have pulled a switch. There must have been two Christianities, and we ended up with the boring one!

I remember once travelling from Croydon to Hendon to do some filming for the BBC. A car met me at my house for the two-hour drive through heavy traffic. The driver and I struck up a conversation. He was an ex-footballer and cricketer in his late 50s, and we were getting on like a house on fire right up until the time we arrived at my destination. As I was getting out of the car, he asked, 'What programme are you making, anyway?'

'*Songs of Praise*,' I told him.

'Oh, God!' he cried out instinctively. 'Not you! You don't look the type!' In just three little words, I lost all my credibility in his eyes.

Perhaps times have changed. That was then and this is now. Christianity was exciting and relevant in the old days, but things are different now.

The adventure continues

Yet Christians are *still* dying for their faith in many parts of the world even today. In the old Soviet Union, in China, in Latin America, and in parts of Africa and the Middle East, Christians are killed every year because they dare to take a stand for what they believe in.

This is odd. Because, let's face it, nobody goes to the bother of killing people for holding irrelevant and outdated beliefs. We laugh at those who still consider the sun to be a god. We pity those who think that the moon hangs in the night sky. We ignore those who warn that planes can't possibly fly.

We don't kill people who have every record Des O'Connor ever produced; we consider that to be punishment enough in itself. We humour them. We find them funny. Or sad. Or both. What we *don't* do is take them out and shoot them.

So there has to be more to Christianity than the irrelevant and antiquated religion we so often see. There has to be more than meets the eye.

3
Experienced God seeks employment

OF COURSE, there are those who consider a belief in God, or in the existence of God, to be deeply irrational. 'What you see is what you get,' they argue, 'and *that's all folks!* Science has disproved religion.'

In olden times, they say, people believed in magic and witchcraft. They believed in miracles and the supernatural. People used to think that birds could fly because God held them in the sky. They used to think that apples fell from trees because God pushed them. There was simply no other explanation. But now we understand that all this has more to do with aeronautics and gravity than with God. We have outgrown the need for God: he is quite simply redundant.

A God of the gaps

When Soviet cosmonaut Yuri Gagarin became the first man in space in 1961, he declared that (roughly translated)

'God's not in!' God, we tell ourselves, was an idea for primitive peoples. It was a convenient theory to explain things we didn't understand. Now we just don't need it anymore.

But is a belief in God so irrational? If science really has replaced Christian faith, then why are so many scientists Christians? From what we're told, you would think that owning a white coat and walking into a laboratory would soon cure you for ever of a belief in the supernatural.

Yet the truth is that many scientists are so astounded by the complexity of the universe that they look for an architect behind it. And it's not just Christians who do this. They find the idea that the universe happened by accident about as convincing as the idea that an explosion in a scrap metal yard could produce a perfect working model of a Rolls Royce Silver Shadow with a full tank of petrol and the keys in the ignition.

Everything you ever wanted to know about . . .

A few years ago, I went with my wife to an exhibition of artwork by the painter Renoir at the National Gallery. There was a big display about his most famous painting, 'Umbrellas'. Experts had X-rayed it to determine exactly how it had been painted. What they found was that Renoir had either changed his mind halfway through, or he had made a mistake. The woman in the corner of the picture, for instance, had started life as a man. I came away from the exhibition feeling that I knew everything there was to know about how Renoir painted 'Umbrellas'. But knowing *how* 'Umbrellas' was painted didn't make me lose interest in who had painted it; in fact, it made me more interested in Renoir than I ever had been before.

And it's the same thing with God. Science can tell us how the world was created; but it cannot tell us who or what was responsible. These are entirely different questions, but both are equally important.

If top-level scientists can speculate about the nature of the universe and still believe the Bible, then there has to be more to Christianity than an irrational crutch which allows the ignorant of the world to make it through the day. There must be more than meets the eye.

4

If it feels good . . .

WHEN you think of Christianity, what do you think of?

Well, most people think of a long list of *do*s and *don't*s: with more *don't*s than *do*s. Thou shalt not do anything enjoyable. Thou shalt not have any fun. Ever. Amen. In fact, 'Thou shalt not . . .' is one of the Bible's best-known phrases.

Most of us seem to think that Christianity is too strict. It's out of date.

Is it fun? Then stop it!

Take sex, for example. A friend of mine remembers being told by his vicar when he was young, 'Sex is dirty, degrading and disgusting. So save it for your wife!'

We often think of God as a miserable old geezer with a twisted sense of humour. It's as though he looked down from heaven, listed all the things we enjoyed doing, and outlawed them all. So we settle instead for a much more practical approach to life: 'If it feels good, do it'. This has become the guiding principle of our day. 'What's right for you is right for you,' we argue, 'but it may not be right for me. And I would never impose my own standards on you, so don't you judge me.'

Tolerance and freedom are the watchwords of our generation. Do what you want, as long as you don't hurt anyone and as long as you're sincere about it.

Why accept everything the Bible has to say about morality, hook, line and sinker? Be open-minded. Pick'n'mix a bit. It's far more sensible to choose your own morals than to have them pushed on you.

Boomerang!

But today, there's evidence of a backlash: it seems as though everyone's talking about what's wrong with our society. We lament the moral vacuum into which we've been sucked, and we call for a return to a clearer idea of right and wrong. Our politicians plead for a return to traditional family values which they seem unable to deliver: 'Back to basics'. So we demand their resignation when they engage in little 'indiscretions'.

'If it feels good, do it' has proved to be a disastrous policy. So maybe there's more to Christian morality than meets the eye.

5

'I still haven't found what I'm looking for'

PEOPLE think that the Church is boring, irrelevant, irrational, and a massive killjoy; yet every day thousands and thousands of people around the world become Christians.

The idea that the Church is dying is badly misguided – in fact, it's growing faster than ever. Around the world a staggering 100,000 people make the decision to become Christians and join the Church *every day!* And it's not just the Church which is growing. Since the late 1960s, and particularly in recent years, we have experienced a 'spiritual awakening'. There has been an increasing awareness amongst all sorts of people that they are not just flesh and bone. There has to be some kind of soul or spirit which makes us what we are.

So what on earth could persuade 100,000 people a day to turn their lives upside down, often at great personal cost, by becoming Christians?

God is dead, and I'm not feeling too good either

We have become aware that all of our science has failed to produce the paradise we're after. As Bono of the band U2 sang, 'I still haven't found what I'm looking for'. We have been sold a crock. We have bought a cure for baldness and discovered that the salesman is as bald as a coot!

In fact, the very technology we thought would give us the answers we needed has merely added to our problems. It's as though the world has suddenly woken up to the fact that science is not our saviour. The idea that God is dead has itself been pronounced terminally ill.

We can see evidence of this in the rising popularity of horoscopes, Eastern mysticism, tarot cards, crystals, palm reading, meditation techniques, and the popularity of the whole New Age movement. And it's not just a bunch of weirdos and hippies who are buying into this kind of philosophy; it's bank managers and housewives, teachers, lawyers, athletes, accountants and builders. It's your neighbour; it may even be you. It's people from every sphere of life.

More than meets the eye

We seem to be aware that, as Martin Luther King put it, 'The great things in this universe are things that we never see.' We seem instinctively to know that there is more to life than we've been told. There is a new and genuine hunger for spiritual things, an overwhelming sense of confusion about what is true and what is not.

People say, 'Any belief will do, just as long as you are *sincere*, and you don't hurt anybody.' This is the modern ethos. All religions are basically the same: they just have different brand names.

'It seemed like a good idea at the time'

But is this true? After all, I can be *sincere* in believing that gargling with arsenic every morning is a good thing for my health, but I'll still be dead within a month.

When I was about 20, I was part of an obscure and now very defunct rock band. On one occasion we travelled from London to Uckfield to do a gig, and afterwards the organisers put us on the last train out of the station. We all believed sincerely that we were bound for London . . . right up until the train pulled into Eastbourne. We had to spend the entire night, until 6am, shivering on the station platform.

It's important to be sincere, but you can be sincerely wrong or sincerely right. The important question is: Is it true?

Most people agree that there is more to life than meets the eye.

Part Two

To Begin at the Beginning

6

The roof of the Sistine Chapel

I REMEMBER the story of the little girl who asked her mother, 'Mummy, is God everywhere?'

'Yes, darling,' replied the mother.

'Is God in the kitchen with us now, mummy?'

'Yes, darling. God is with us now.'

'Mummy, if God is with us in this room, is he on the table?'

'Yes, darling,' said the mother, hesitantly.

'If God is on the table, is he in this glass then, mummy?'

'Yes, I suppose so, poppet. God is everywhere, so he must be in that glass.'

'Got him!' cried the girl, turning the glass swiftly upside down as though catching a fly.

God is probably not how you imagine him to be. He is not a big old man living in the clouds, as Michelangelo pictured him for the roof of the Vatican's famous Sistine Chapel.

'The force be with you'

When Moses asked God for a description of himself, God gave a strange reply. He said, 'I just am.' God has always existed, is everywhere, knows everything, and can do anything.

Now that's not the easiest thing in the world to understand. We all want to pin God down, defining him as this or that. But if God 'just is', then he defies this kind of pigeon-holing.

But if God is not an old man, neither is he an impersonal force. We sometimes picture God as a kind of cosmic power source that we can tap into just like Luke Skywalker in *Star Wars*: as though all we have to do is to say, 'The force be with you,' and . . . hey presto! We are plugged in as easily as plugging into the Internet.

Out of sight, out of mind

The film *Pascali's Island* is about a government spy in turn-of-the-century Turkey. Recruited during a time of trouble, Basil Pascali is still writing regular reports back to his employers some twenty years later. He never hears from them, and he does not really question why. Unknown to him, officials have not read his letters in years. No one in government service even knows that he exists. The only reason he is still paid is that no one ever thought to cancel his monthly cheque. Yet out of a sense of devoted loyalty, Pascali continues his activities as a spy for his remote and distant monarch.

Because we cannot see God, and few of us hear voices, we can be tempted to think of God like Pascali's employers: unknown, unseen, remote.

But in fact, the whole of the Bible – God's instruction manual for human beings – is the story of people's close relationships with God. He is often referred to as the God of Abraham, of Isaac and Jacob, of Joseph and his 'Amazing Technicolour Dreamcoat'.

God constantly takes a personal interest in people.

7

In God's kitchen

THE BEGINNING seems like a good place to start: the very beginning.

In the beginning, God created the world. The truth is that nobody knows for sure how the world began, or when. Most scientists nowadays subscribe to the so-called 'Big Bang Theory', in which the entire universe was created when a single giant photon of light exploded in the first moment of time.

It's all terribly confusing, and in none of the different variations of the theory does anybody have any answers as to *why* the photon should have exploded in the first place. We just have to take it on faith.

Before the Big Bang Theory, most scientists and scholars seem to have agreed that God made the world; they just disagreed about how long it took.

Well, I'll be a monkey's uncle!

A friend of mine once took part in a radio debate, defending his view that God had created the world. His opponent was an atheist, ardently opposed to the Christian view of creation on the grounds that it made no sense.

'This man is a Christian,' he said of my friend, 'and he wants you to believe that God created the world out of nothing, which is ridiculous.'

'And this man,' replied my friend, 'is an atheist; he wants you to believe that nothing created the world out of nothing, which is even more ridiculous.'

In June 1860, during the British Association debate, Bishop of Oxford 'Soapy Sam' Wilberforce put down a prominent biologist and follower of Darwin's theory of evolution, T. H. Huxley, with the quip, 'Let me ask Mr Huxley just one question: is it through his grandfather or his grandmother that he claims descent from a monkey?' The crowd loved it. But although he won the battle, 'Soapy Sam' lost the war.

Most people now believe in some form of evolution. And this includes many Christians.

God's chemistry set

Christians believe that God made the world. Exactly how is not so important: we may never know how precisely the world was made. But as we've already seen, How? and Why? are very different questions.

Christians also believe that God knew what he was doing when he created the world. As Einstein said, 'God does not play dice.' He was not experimenting with a massive chemistry set and creating things accidentally. It was an ordered and deliberate process, and it turned out just as he had intended. The first chapter of Genesis, the first book of the Bible, ends with God looking at everything he'd made and saying, 'It's good!'

8

The meaning of life

LIFE IS more than just existence: it has meaning. The big question is: What?

Douglas Adams, in *The Hitchhiker's Guide to the Galaxy*, tried his hardest to convince us that the answer to this question was really 42. But most of us are hoping that there's a bit more to it than that! If you don't believe in God, though, it's hard to see what life is all about.

For some people, life is just a biological accident. Famous for his wit, Mark Twain nevertheless remarked, 'Men are born, they labour and sweat and struggle; they squabble and scold and fight; those they love are taken from them, and the joy of life is turned to aching grief. The release comes at last and they vanish from a world where they were of no consequence . . . a world which will lament them a day and forget them for ever.'

The poet Philip Larkin considered life to be nothing more than 'slow dying'. His fear of life and the sense of despair it brought him was matched only by his fear of death.

But if you believe that God exists, then life already has meaning. Your job is not to invent a meaning for life; it is, rather, to discover what that meaning is, and then to do something about it.

Finding your way

A friend of mine was once travelling on the London Underground. She was amused by the behaviour of another traveller, a businessman. This man spent the entire journey studying the tube map in his diary and comparing it with the names on the station platforms. Eventually, realising that the man was hopelessly lost, my friend moved over and sat next to him, offering to help. It was at that point that she realised why the man was lost. Not only was he German, with little grasp of the English language, but his diary was French and the map in the front was of the Paris Metro!

Unless you're holding the right map, you're going to get lost. If it's God's world we live in, and we act as though he's not there, life will never make sense.

How many people spend the first half of their life gazing into their future and saying, 'You wait 'til I leave school/pass my driving test/get a rise/get married/get a Ferrari – then I'll really be living!' And they spend the second half reliving the past and saying, 'I remember when the streets were safe/petrol was cheap/people dressed

properly/music was music/politicians could be trusted –
those were the days!'

It's as though we spend half our lives staggering up a
mountain and the other half rolling down the other side.
We pass the summit by with no idea why we were on the
mountain in the first place.

9

The world should not be the way it is

ACCORDING to the Bible, God says that life is meant to be good. It's meant to be wholesome and fulfilling, creative and eternal. It doesn't take a genius to see that this is not the way things actually are.

Marriages are breaking up and becoming as disposable as McDonalds' wrappers. Streets in which it was once safe to leave the front doors unlocked have become crime scenes. Suicide rates are constantly rising; so are rape statistics. The poor are undoubtedly getting poorer whilst the rich get richer. There are never fewer than forty wars going on in the world at any one time. Irreplaceable rain forests are being cut down, and endangered species are dying out at the rate of three a day.

The world should not be the way it is: that much is obvious. So what went wrong?

Enter Adam and Eve, stage right

The Bible says that when God created people, he gave them the gift of choice. In other words, he gave them a say in how their lives and the whole world turned out.

He could have created a world without choice: a world where everyone and everything behaved exactly as they were programmed to do. But in that case, he would have ended up with a world filled with robots. Or zombies. With no freedom, and therefore no real life. And where's the fun in that?

Will you be my Valentine?

Every year, I give my wife a Valentine's Day present. Each year I rack my brains trying to come up with something original so that it's a real surprise. I don't give her a present because I *have* to; I give it because I *want* to. Hopefully, it's because she knows that I *choose* to express my love for her in this way, that makes the gift valuable to her. (Which is just as well, because what I come up with is usually rather sorry and meagre!) If I gave her something because I was programmed to do so and had no choice, it would mean nothing to her.

What makes any gift valuable is the fact that it is freely given. The giver is not obliged to buy it. They won't short circuit and explode if they don't.

In the New Testament, John, who was one of Jesus' first followers, tells us that God is a God of love. To a God of love, a world with no choice is unthinkable, because you can only love somebody *by choice*. So choice is the greatest gift we have.

Whose stupid idea was this?

The problem with choices, of course, is that it is possible to make the wrong ones. And this is exactly what old Adam and Eve did in the book of Genesis. By choosing to ignore God, they made the mother of all bad decisions.

When you love somebody, you hope that they will choose to love you in return. But you can never guarantee it. So you open yourself up to the possibility of being rejected by them. Love involves taking risks, because you cannot force another person to love you back, no matter how deeply you love them.

We don't have to look far in the world around us to see that little has changed since Adam and Eve. There are still people who put their own interests ahead of the interests of others. There are still people who take what they want regardless of the consequences. And none of us are immune from making some *very* bad judgments.

10

Whatever happened to sin?

SMALL mistakes can have big consequences, as an old rhyme illustrates:

> For want of a nail, the shoe was lost;
> For want of a shoe, the horse was lost;
> For want of a horse, the rider was lost;
> For want of a rider, the message was lost;
> For want of a message, the battle was lost;
> And all for the want of a horse-shoe nail.

All choices have consequences. Good choices have good consequences, and bad choices have bad consequences.

Because God loves us, he's given us some good advice on which choices to make; and he's given us the freedom to make whichever choices we like.

It's like the business traveller and his map of the Paris Metro. If he'd had a map of the London tube, he still might not have taken the right route. Having the map helps, but it doesn't ensure that we will follow it.

It's a sin!

We often have the wrong idea about sin. We sometimes think that anything we really enjoy doing must automatically be a sin. We remember the adverts: 'Fresh cream cakes – naughty . . . but nice!' We use expressions like, 'That's so good, it's a sin!'

It might help us at this point to clarify things by making a quick definition. *Something is a sin because it is damaging and destructive, not damaging and destructive because it is a sin.*

We all know about the Ten Commandments, for instance: Thou shalt not kill, steal, commit adultery, bear false witness, covet thy neighbour's ox, etc. And most of us agree that they are a pretty good rough guide to morality (even if we suspect that God is really something of a killjoy, out to ruin everybody's fun!) Like the tube map, which shows how to get from one place to another in the simplest way, the Ten Commandments are basically a matter of common sense. Breaking them is a bad choice because it brings in its wake bad consequences.

It's a personal thing

We all know the story of Charles Dickens' *A Christmas Carol*. Scrooge's selfishness and greed trap and imprison him. In the end, he doesn't control his money so much as his money controls him. It's only when he is shown a vision of his own future that the true consequences of his behaviour come home to him; and he is set free by learning to be generous.

The price tag for greed is misery. A friend of mine found this out to his cost a few years ago. His good looks made him very attractive to women, and in spite of the fact that he was married with two children, he had a number of affairs which remained undiscovered for several years. But inevitably he was found out. As a result, he lost the love of his wife and the respect of his children. He now lives alone, starved of the affection of the three people in the world who matter to him the most.

'A pair of star-cross'd lovers'

Sin has consequences. In the New Testament, the Apostle Paul says that the wages of sin is death. This might sound a little melodramatic, but all it means is that sin is destructive. And not just to the person who sins: the Bible notes that the consequences of sin can last three or four generations.

In Shakespeare's famous play, *Romeo and Juliet*, Romeo loves Juliet and Juliet loves Romeo. All they want to do is get married and spend the rest of their lives staring lovingly into each other's eyes, breaking only for the occasional game of tonsil hockey. Everything *should* be wonderful, but of course it's not. Romeo is a Montague and Juliet is a Capulet, and the Montague and Capulet families hate each other. No one can really remember why: they just seem always to have hated each other. As a result, Romeo and Juliet are destroyed by the sins of their parents. As the result of a terrible misunderstanding, they both kill themselves.

Just when you thought it was safe to go back into the water. . .

Of course, if God made us and loves us, then he must surely know what's best for us. If we choose to turn our backs on God and his advice, then we and those around us will have to face the consequences.

Picture this: before you stands a wide and deserted beach leading into a deep blue sea. The climate is warm, the sand is soft, the sea is calm, and birds are singing as the palm trees sway gently in the wind. It all looks too good to be true. And of course it is. In the middle of the beach is a large sign: SHARK INFESTED WATERS: NO SWIMMING. I go swimming and get eaten by a shark. I have no one to blame but myself, because I ignored the advice.

All of this is a long and complicated way of saying that the world is not the way it should be, and this is predominantly *our* fault.

11

Global meltdown

THIS HAS never been more clear than now. We know that the majority of the problems people face all over the planet could be solved if we really wanted them to be, and were prepared actually to do something about them.

But it's not just humanity that is affected by human sin. The present ecological crisis, with serious deforestation and a depletion of the outer ozone layer, may be causing global warming and a shift in the earth's delicate eco-system. But it has human greed and shortsightedness as its cause. Trees which have stood for a hundred years or more are being cleared to make way for cattle grazing land, or mines for precious metals. Holes are punched in the ozone layer, and asthma affects increasing numbers of people because we want the convenience of personal travel in our own cars.

Even so-called 'natural' disasters like earthquakes usually have human sin or negligence at the root of their devastation. Compare the recent earthquake in Los Angeles with those in Mexico City, Maharashtra (India) and Kobe (Japan). Look closely and you will see that poverty and poor housing claim the most lives. Had Kobe been as well equipped against earthquakes as Tokyo, in terms of building design and materials, far fewer of its five thousand victims would have died. And the 1993 earthquake in India claimed roughly five times as many lives as Kobe, in spite of the fact that it registered almost a full point lower on the Richter scale.

One single owner, no problem neighbours

I remember travelling to India to see the remains of some of the 66 villages utterly destroyed by the earthquake. In one, I saw everything flattened except for a single house, which belonged to a rich man. It was the only properly-built house in the village. Everything else had totally collapsed, crushing the inhabitants. Yet this house didn't even have a crack in the plaster. Nothing could have demonstrated more forcefully the gap in fortunes between the rich and poor. And yet, like the ruins around it, this house was standing empty. Dependent upon the villagers for his livelihood, the rich owner had had to abandon his spacious and modern villa when the villagers moved a few miles down the road.

Martin Luther King remarked that none of us are independent: we are all *interdependent*. And the sins of one affect the lives of others. None of us lives in a vacuum.

Passing the buck

Nevertheless, we seem to be very reluctant to take the responsibility for what we have done, and to carry the can for our mistakes. When something goes wrong, we usually look for someone else to blame. We don't like to admit when we make mistakes. My mum tells me that when I was young, like most children, I went through a phase of lying. I would do something wrong, and then deny that I had done it, even if she had seen me do it: and, most stupidly, even if I knew that she had seen me do it.

In fact, some of our worst mistakes are made trying to cover up other, lesser mistakes. There is something in us that just doesn't want to admit that we've done wrong. It's an old trick. Adam did it, and he blamed Eve. Eve did it, and she blamed the snake. And the snake, as the old joke goes, didn't have a leg to stand on.

'The buck stops here'

The press dubbed the US Iran-Contra affair during the 1980s, 'Irangate'. Like the American public, the press loved Colonel Oliver North, in spite of his illegal activities. He was handsome and he looked good on television. And besides, he was 'just following orders'. They loved Fawn Hall, his beautiful assistant. She also looked good on television and was 'just following orders'. But they hated

Admiral Poindexter, North's boss. He wasn't beautiful, didn't look good on television, and was not 'just following orders'. Yet he was the one who took the rap for the mistakes of his juniors. (And who knows, perhaps even for the President.) When he declared, 'The buck stops here', he was very much the exception rather than the rule.

The rule is, 'If at all possible, blame someone else; if not, blame God'.

'I'm sorry, God's in a meeting right now'

Christians claim that God is all-knowing, all-seeing and all-powerful. They say that he is able to be everywhere, and is consumed with love for us. So why on earth doesn't he *do* something about the terrible state of the world today? Even if we admit that it is *our* fault that the world is in such a terrible state in the first place, we still want to know what God is going to do about it. Perhaps he doesn't know about it, or doesn't care, or perhaps he just can't do anything about it. Otherwise he would have *done* something, surely.

Well, Christians believe that God *has* done something about it. Read on.

Part Three

The Life and Death of
Jesus Christ

12

'FAB, Scott!'

ALTHOUGH he was not to blame, it was time for God to do something: to come to our rescue. What God decided to do was to take the buck himself. To do this, he became a human being. The consequence of sin is death, and in order to take this consequence upon himself, it was necessary to become mortal. And the person that God became in order to come to our rescue was Jesus.

'Thunderbirds are go!'

I used to love watching *Thunderbirds*, even though the basic plot of each episode was more or less the same. A city is being rocked by an earthquake. Meanwhile, half a dozen coastal villages are devastated by a tidal wave. A five-mile oil slick destroys wildlife when a massive tanker, pelted by the tidal wave, runs aground. Dense clouds cover the sky, turning day into night. Outlying towns are deluged when a river bursts its flood banks. On the hillsides, sheep grow extra heads when the earthquake causes a nuclear power station to leak. Mountain areas are eaten up by forest fires. The North Pole starts to melt. Brains loses his glasses. And Virgil can't find the keys to Thunderbird 2!

Nevertheless, by some miracle or other, by the end of 25 minutes everything is set to rights. Thunderbirds to the rescue! International Rescue save the planet . . . again!

Roughly translated, the name 'Jesus' simply means 'God to the Rescue'. And the time when God decided to come to our rescue was, of course, Christmas.

Christmas — the movie

We all know the Christmas story, the story of Jesus' birth: at least, we think we do. The inn, the stable, the wise men, the cattle, the shepherds, the star, the presents, the carols and a warm, glowing sensation inside. But how much of this is actually true?

We are aware that Hollywood glamorises and distorts everything. For example, if Martin Scorcese or Steven Spielberg were given $100 million to do a movie version of the Christmas story, what would they make of it?

To begin with, the whole thing would no doubt be done on an epic scale, more like *Lawrence of Arabia* than *Dr Who*. Dramatic landscapes would be captured with soft focus camerawork, and a dozen choirs would combine to perform the Oscar-winning John Williams soundtrack. Big stars would be drafted in, even for the small parts. Sean Connery would be cast as the innkeeper, with Michelle Pfieffer as his wife. Jack Nicholson would be evil King Herod. Charlton Heston, Marlon Brando and Bill Cosby would come out of retirement to play the Wise Men. Harrison Ford and Kevin Costner would play shepherds. Woody Allen would play a sheep.

The stable and the animals would be specially cleaned up for the occasion, with hay smelling of Chanel No 5 and a host of people employed with poop scoops to ensure that nobody stepped in something unsavoury. The casting sessions for the cows alone would take a week! The crib, constructed from antique oak by a team of skilled New England carpenters, would be expertly lit to bring out the right tones.

A group from Disney would be on hand at all times to advise on getting that wholesome family atmosphere, and *Star Wars* director George Lucas would co-ordinate the special effects. The women's clothes would be designed by Bruce Oldfield, the men's by Calvin Klein. Shares in toothpaste would rise on the Wall Street stock exchange.

'Little Lord Jesus, no crying he makes'

The funny thing is that, although Hollywood has a well-earned reputation for replacing accuracy with glamour, they couldn't possibly make the nativity scene any less real to us than it is now. We already think of Jesus being born after an easy labour, and being placed in delicate blankets in a brand-new Mothercare crib. We already imagine the parents, the cattle, the shepherds, the sheep, the visitors, and even the stars smiling. Everyone hums *Away in a Manger* and the baby Jesus gurgles contentedly.

But the birth of Jesus, God's Christmas present to the world, was actually a much more brutal affair. To begin with, Mary had to make a journey of seventy miles, from Nazareth to Bethlehem, on the back of a mule, although she was very heavily pregnant. She and Joseph arrived in Bethlehem, the home town of Joseph's ancestors, in order to be registered in a nationwide population census.

And when they got there, they discovered the town so packed that all the 'hotels' were full. Joseph was so poor that he couldn't afford the bribe to get his pregnant fiancée a room, even though she was ready to go into labour. Instead, the couple stayed in a cattle shed – little more than a cave, really – and Jesus' first bed was the animals' feeding trough. The smell coming from the cattle, the birth, the sweaty shepherds and the dung, in such a confined space, must have been almost unbearable. Hardly the cosy affair we usually imagine at that time of year!

Strange but true?

So how well do we actually know the Christmas story? How well can we distinguish the truth from the various myths and stories that have built up over the years? For instance, did you know that:

- Nobody knows the exact date of Jesus' birth. But we can say for sure that it was not 25th December because the sheep were still out in the fields. Had it been December, both sheep and shepherds would have been frozen solid!

- Celebrating Christmas dates from around AD336. It was held in December to coincide with the Roman pagan festival of the Sun.

- There were not 'Three Kings' present at Jesus' birth. In fact, according to the Bible there were no kings at all! There was just an unspecified number of foreign academics. And according to tradition, they did not arrive until some time after the birth, by which time the shepherds would have been long gone.

- These boffins made a terrible blunder. Expecting a king, they arrived at the palace of King Herod. Herod governed Judea under Roman authority and he was not pleased to discover that a rival king had been born. He ordered the death of every Jewish male in the area under the age of 2. Warned in a dream, Joseph and his new family fled into Egypt.

- The first Christmas card was sent in 1843.

- Carols were originally festival dance tunes in the Middle Ages. They were repopularised and sung in the streets during Queen Victoria's reign.

- Prince Albert introduced the Christmas tree from Germany.

- Christmas crackers were originally parcels of sweets wrapped up for children. They made their way across the Channel from France and have ended up on the modern Christmas dinner table.

- Christmas became a big festival only in the last century. In fact, most of the traditions we cherish about Christmas date from the time of Charles Dickens! No wonder his book *A Christmas Carol* is so popular!

The truth and anything but the truth

It makes you think, doesn't it, just how easy it is to get the wrong end of the stick about things?

I recently went to an important business meeting in the City of London. As I got into the half-crowded lift to go up to the right floor, I noticed that I was the only person casually dressed and not wearing a suit. Just as the doors were closing, an anxious-looking man rushed in. Inspecting me carefully, he stated rather loudly, 'You must be the lift engineer!' Since I was not dressed formally, he assumed that I was a technician. Not seeing past my appearance, he got entirely the wrong end of the stick.

It's the same with Christmas. There's a lot more to it than meets the eye. But not seeing past appearances, we have got entirely the wrong end of the stick. We have invented all sorts of myths and traditions about Christmas which have nothing to do with the Bible or the real Christmas story at all.

And if we've picked up the wrong end of the stick as far as Christmas is concerned, what have we made of the rest of Jesus' life?

13

The man who was God

MOST people have a stained-glass window image of Jesus. He is conveniently floating a few inches above ground level, with a 'ring of confidence' above his head like an overgrown Polo mint! He's always pictured as thin, white, blond and a bit pale and pasty. He usually has a small animal asleep at his feet. Basically, he looks as though he's never done a hard day's work in his life. You get the impression that he would have been bullied at school.

When I was a kid, I based my view of Jesus entirely on the endless number of stained-glass windows I had seen. In the end, I became convinced that Jesus was really the greensman for a cricket club, since he always seemed to be standing in front of a perfectly mown lawn!

But as with Christmas, it really isn't like this.

Feet on the ground

The Bible says that although Jesus was truly and wholly God, he became a *real* human being. He didn't float above the earth's surface; instead, he was faced with all the same problems and obstacles you and I have to deal with. For instance, in the New Testament, Jesus cries. He is anxious. He is stressed. He is angry. He is happy. He experiences despair. He tells jokes. He even falls asleep in times of crisis! And although it's never mentioned in the Bible, we can safely assume that he also went to the toilet!

We create for ourselves a stained-glass image of Jesus, and then consign him to the realms of Peter Pan and the tooth fairy. He wanders around almost surreally, never quite touching base with reality. Yet the truth is a long way from this image.

'Who does he think he is?'

Jesus grew up in the despised north of his country. He lived in obscurity as a carpenter's son. His life as a public figure did not begin until he was about 30. When he started preaching, the people in his village didn't take him seriously. 'That's old Joe's son, isn't it?' they said to each other. 'Who does he think he is, telling us that he's on a mission to save the world?'

In the late 1970s, the rock singer John Mellencamp was a

bright young thing with the ink still wet on his first record deal. The record company insisted that he change his name to *Johnny Cougar*: they thought that it would attract sales. The company pulled out all the stops to promote their new heart-throb. But his small home town was less impressed. Not fooled by the hype, one neighbour refused to let her son buy a Johnny Cougar T-shirt. He lived down the street. She knew his mother. 'I'm not going to spend $10 on a picture of little Johnny Mellencamp,' she told her son!

The people from Jesus' home town understood that he was a real human being. But they had problems with the idea that he was different. We understand that Jesus was different; but we have problems with the idea that he was a real human being.

'I can resist everything except temptation'

One of the New Testament writers remarks that Jesus was tempted 'in every way', yet he was able to resist this temptation to do wrong. We are also told that he was tempted to abuse his relationship with God to further his own interests and to save his own skin. This must have seemed particularly attractive when the Romans sentenced him to death. But Jesus adamantly refused to give in to these temptations.

During the hurricane of 1988, a lot of trees near where I live fell down because they were unable to resist the force of the wind. Yet some did remain standing throughout the storm. They withstood more of an onslaught than those which blew over and 'gave in' to the wind. It's the same with Jesus. It's just because he was able to stand against the full force of temptation without giving in that we know he understands what it's really like for us. Because when you stop to think about it, it's only the person who overcomes temptation and doesn't cave in to it that really experiences the full force of its power.

Although he was as human as we are, Jesus chose to live life God's way, rather than his own way.

14

Tick as appropriate

Ask almost anyone who Jesus was. Nine times out of ten, they'll tell you virtually the same thing: Jesus was basically a good bloke. He was loving, kind, honest, gentle, generous, thoughtful and selfless. A good man. A good moral teacher.

However, the writer and academic, C. S. Lewis, argued that whatever a person thought about Jesus, the one conclusion they could not come to was that he was a good man. Why? Because a good man, especially a religious man, would never claim to be God. And that's exactly what Jesus did claim.

Logically, therefore, Jesus had to be either a whole lot *more* or a whole lot *less* than good.

The options

In fact, there are only three possible explanations about who Jesus was:

- he was a con-man who lied and cheated his way into power and lasting recognition;
- he was as one card short of a full deck; or
- he was exactly what he claimed.

Jesus was a Jew who broke the sabbath. He rioted in the temple. He condemned the religious authorities of his day for being corrupt and hypocritical. He claimed to have been given the divine power to forgive sins. And finally, he admitted to being the unique Son of God.

'Don't let's come up with any patronising nonsense about his being a great human teacher,' C. S. Lewis concluded. 'He hasn't left that open to us. He didn't intend to.'

So was Jesus nothing more than an accomplished con-man, or a deluded fool? Or was he, just possibly, who he claimed to be?

Rabbits, hats and five thousand for dinner

Why do people become con artists? What motivates someone deliberately to deceive others? There can only be one possible answer to this: profit.

For instance, some years ago a Frenchman succeeded in selling the Eiffel Tower for scrap! Printing off some official-looking headed notepaper, he wrote to several Paris scrap metal merchants. He informed them that he was authorised by the French government to dispose of the famous monument. Each of them was keen to close the deal. And astonishingly, they all paid up, unaware of their competitors. The first they knew of the deception was when they all turned up to dismantle it . . . on the same day! By which time, of course, their money and its new guardian were well on their way to America, where he no doubt tried to sell the Brooklyn Bridge.

If this is a good example of a con-man, how does Jesus compare? Well, everyone is agreed that he was kind, selfless, caring and considerate. He spent his whole life putting other people ahead of himself. Not once did he ask for money. When he finally died on the cross, penniless and ridiculed, the only thing he had left of any value was his robe – and the soldiers who executed him gambled this away.

If Jesus was a con-man, his lack of success is remarkable. In fact, he deserves a place in the *Guinness Book of Records* for his total incompetence.

Famous for fifteen minutes

But what if he just wanted to be remembered? What if the whole thing was just a publicity stunt cooked up to get him his fifteen minutes of fame?

Well, if he was after fame, he went about it in a very strange way. He came from an obscure town in an obscure country; he spoke an obscure language. If he'd had any sense, he'd have headed for the big city. He'd have hired a publicist. He'd have done something spectacular.

Had he been interested in fame, Jesus would have gone to Rome, the throbbing centre of the Roman Empire. Or Athens, the cultural centre of the ancient world. Yet Jesus stayed where he was. And when he did do extraordinary things, he told people not to publicise it. In fact, Jesus would have been a modern advertising agency's nightmare. The one person he didn't seem to be interested in was himself. Pretty odd behaviour for someone who wanted his moment of fame.

So it seems unlikely that Jesus was a con-man. After all, what could he possibly hope to gain?

One raisin short of a fruitcake

So what if he was a nutcase? It is, if you think about it, pretty strange to say things that lead people to believe that you think you are the unique Son of God, the creator of all that is and ever has been.

In one of London's big teaching hospitals, there used to be a patient who genuinely believed that he was God Almighty. The fact that he also considered himself and his every movement to be controlled by the BBC shouldn't detract from his claim: it would have been unbelievable even without this extra wrinkle.

Virtually any claim to be God seems ridiculous; and people who follow people who claim to be God seem to be ridiculous as well.

So are Christians a bunch of fools, the disciples of a madman? Was Jesus a candidate for 'Care in the Community'?

It is ironic that whilst some people consider Jesus to have been mad, far more people consider him to have been a good moral teacher. How can an insane man be a good moral teacher? Jesus amazed people with the depth of his intellect and understanding even when he was a boy. The gospels make it very clear that he was an exceptionally intelligent and wise man.

A handle on reality

But did Jesus have a firm grasp of reality? The evidence suggests that he did.

He had an ability to perceive people's problems right away. He could speak with authority and relevance to the situations of people he'd only just met. He had instinctive insight. He spoke with down-to-earth stories and illustrations. He had a knack of communicating with people whatever their station in life.

All of this indicates that he had a better grip on reality than most of the people he met. The picture of Jesus which is painted by the gospels is certainly not one of a lunatic.

So if Jesus wasn't just a good man, and he wasn't a conman, and he wasn't mad, what was he? Well, his followers considered him to be exactly who he claimed to be: the Son of God. But the people who killed him considered him to be a heretic and a dangerous subversive.

15

Public enemy Number One

FROM the very beginning of his public life, Jesus was caught up in bitter controversy. The people in his home town of Nazareth conspired to kill him when he claimed that he had come to bring them freedom. He surrounded himself with what polite society considered to be most unsavoury characters. His closest friends were fishermen, prostitutes, revolutionaries and tax collectors. And he spent most of his time with poor people, traitors, criminals and outcasts.

- Jesus had no time for the official religious leaders. He accused them of 'shutting heaven's doors in peoples' faces'.
- He took liberties with religious rules. He argued that they should be a help to people rather than a hindrance.
- He never trained as a priest, but he amazed people with his knowledge and his insights.
- He flew in the face of accepted practice. He taught

people through telling them stories when everyone else gave people endless dry doctrines to learn parrot-fashion.

You wouldn't think that a message of love could be so controversial. And you certainly wouldn't think that it could be enough to get Jesus killed.

Yet it was.

Martin Luther King

The plain truth is that love is not popular: not *real* love.

Martin Luther King is one of my heroes, partly because he demonstrates the unpopularity of this real love. For all the time that he fought for the civil rights of black men and women in the Southern states of the USA, he was hailed by the rest of America – and the world – as a true American and a great man. They cheered when he won the Nobel Peace Prize. Yet when the legal battle was over in the South and he turned his attention to the injustice and inequalities of the Northern states, the same crowd which had cheered him in 1964 now jeered him in 1965.

The same ideas and convictions which led Martin Luther King to reject violence in his struggle for civil rights, led him to oppose the war in Vietnam. The same sense of outrage which had led him to condemn racial segregation in the South led him to denounce financial segregation in the rest of the country. He began to receive criticism from people who had been staunch supporters just a couple of years earlier. They thought that he had now 'gone too far'. Martin Luther King himself, of course, had not changed one bit: it's just that people came to understand how radical he had always been.

And just as it was not immediately obvious how dangerous Martin Luther King was, so it was not immediately obvious how dangerous Jesus was. After all, a message of peace and love looks all rather jolly until you realise that with love always comes an insistence on justice. The Brazilian Archbishop Helder Câmara realised this when he said, 'When I feed the hungry, they call me a saint. When I ask why the hungry have no food, they call me a communist!'

The bitterest pill

It's a bit like medicine. Effective medicines usually taste horrible. To disguise the taste and to encourage people to take the medicines, they are often coated with something like sugar. Jesus' message of love looked good to people until they got through the sugar coating, at which point it became very hard to swallow.

In 1977, Oscar Romero was appointed Archbishop of San Salvador, the capital city of the little Central American country of El Salvador. His main rival for the job was considered to be just too radical, too politically unstable. Romero was a quiet man, a holy man, a 'safe pair of hands'. Yet the same things which had made him so quiet and holy led Archbishop Romero to denounce the injustice he saw all around him. He quickly became a staunch critic of the country's brutal government, an ardent defender of the poor, and, within three years, a martyr. The sugar coating had worn thin.

Public enemy Number One

So how dangerous was Jesus?

- *To the religious authorities*, someone who persuaded people back to real faith was a godsend. Until, that is, they understood that Jesus considered them as far from real faith as anyone else. And Jesus' idea of being able to have a relationship with God which did not rely upon 'official channels' was threatening. Jesus spotlighted the insecurity and hypocrisy of those who had set themselves up as servants of the people, but who were using their positions of power to further their own interests. They wanted him deader than a doornail. And, of course, those honest people *not* profiting from their religious positions found Jesus' claim that he was the Son of God to be a blasphemy worthy of death.

- *To the secular Jewish authorities*, like King Herod, Jesus seemed initially to be a 'spiritual leader'. They thought he was a man unlikely to upset their careful power-sharing agreement with the Roman army. (Although Palestine, where Jesus lived, was at this time a Roman colony, some self-rule was allowed.) But Jesus was a powerful and charismatic figure. His ability to move and inspire great numbers of people surpassed their own. He was far too dangerous for them to allow him to remain alive.

- *To the Romans,* Jesus must initially have seemed like a dream come true. After all, his message to the Jewish people was, 'Love your enemies'. And who were their enemies? The Romans! Rather than stringing him up, they must have wanted to give him a medal. It took a long time for it to dawn on them that Jesus was a destabilising influence. Only gradually did they realise that he was capable of threatening the carefully and brutally established balance of power. He preached allegiance to God alone. He denied that the Empire and Emperor were the holders of ultimate power. Technically, this was a capital offence. But unless it caused trouble, it was easier for the Roman government to let it go. Jesus did not launch a revolution; in fact, he had no intention of doing so. But his message of love and life were still extremely subversive in the Roman world. This became crystal clear to the Romans only in the last week of his life.

Shoot the messenger!

Jesus' obvious love and sincerity made him popular, and his popularity made him dangerous. Roman colonial governor Pontius Pilate recognised the inherent danger which Jesus represented, but he could not find him guilty of any crime. At first, Jesus had seemed to him to be just a naïve and idealistic dreamer. What changed his mind was the behaviour of the crowd. Ultimately, it was the crowd – the people – which controlled Jesus' fate.

It is an old saying that everyone loves a prophet, but not in their own house. To get too close to a prophet is to come under scrutiny. The crowd turned against Jesus because he reminded them too painfully of their inadequacies; and they disliked this message so much that they conspired to kill the messenger.

I recently had to stay in Glasgow overnight to do some filming for a television programme. I was awoken with a start at 1.30am by the sound of the fire alarm. Since I was staying in a posh hotel, each room had its own alarm bell. My first thought was not for my safety, though. Instead, I put my head under the pillow and wondered how I could shut off the sound: I needed my beauty sleep because I was presenting a show 'live' the next morning. I thought of stuffing a sock into the bell, or cutting the wires. I even thought of attacking the bell with my shoe. In fact, it took quite a long time for me to realise *why* the bell was ringing.

When I finally left my room to make my way to the nearest Fire Exit, I noticed that all the other guests had obviously responded to the alarm with the same lack of urgency. I guessed that they too had initially hoped that by dismantling or destroying the alarm bell, they could make the problem just go away. Our instinctive response to an unwelcome message was to destroy the messenger.

The crowd reacted in exactly the same way, only the alarm bell they heard was Jesus, and they didn't try to silence him with their footwear. They had him crucified.

16

Paid on the nail

THE CONSEQUENCE of sin is death. Nowhere is this more clearly and painfully demonstrated than in the death of Jesus. It was not Jesus' own sin which killed him, however: he died as a consequence of other people's sin.

Jesus was executed by the Roman authorities according to the standard method for common people: crucifixion. The official charge recorded by the gospel writer Luke was treason and tax evasion.

Jesus' crucifixion involved the humiliation of being stripped naked and publicly whipped until his back was raw. After that he was forced to carry his own cross – on a freshly mutilated back and amidst constant jeers – to the place of his execution. There he was nailed to a wooden cross and left to hang until he could no longer summon up the strength to breathe. Death on the cross was due to blood loss and suffocation. It was slow and very painful.

Turn your back

But for Jesus, the physical pain was nothing compared to the emotional pain he suffered. The crowd he had loved and supported had rejected him. The disciples who had been his constant companions for three years deserted him and denied all knowledge of him. And to complete the rejection, he was abandoned by God the Father. To a large extent, it was this emotional torture which killed Jesus. He lasted only six hours on the cross – brief by crucifixion standards.

The death of Jesus – the death of the Son of God – shows the lengths to which God the Father was prepared to go to restore his relationship with human beings. It shows the completeness with which he was prepared to pay the price of human sin.

The consequence of sin is death. In the crucifixion, God took this consequence upon himself.

'Someone like that!'

There is a story told about an American army captain in the Vietnam War. Dropped with his men into the jungle, it didn't take him long to realise that they were caught in the middle of an ambush. Recalling his platoon to the clearing, he became aware that they were one man short. Packed into the helicopter, he made a split-second decision to go back for the soldier, who was by now crawling toward them. He was shot in the leg. Dragging him to the chopper, the captain helped him on board. But, at the last moment, as he was clambering on board himself, a burst of gunfire from the trees cut him down where he stood. As the helicopter lifted off, he lay dead in the clearing.

Back in America after the war, the captain's parents decided that they wanted to meet the boy whose life had been spared at the cost of their only son. When he eventually turned up at their home for a meal, one hour late, the soldier shocked and offended the captain's parents with his rudeness and his total lack of gratitude or respect for their son. When he finally left, the captain's mother fell to the floor. Heartbroken, she cried out to God. 'Why? Why did my son have to die for someone like that? Why did he have to die for someone as rude and selfish as that?'

On the cross, Jesus asked a similar question: 'Why? Why have you deserted me, God?' Yet even as he spoke, Jesus knew the answer.

17

'That will do nicely, sir...'

THE OTHER day, I received a credit card application in the post. Nothing but the best: a gold card. In spite of the fact that I don't even own a credit card, and haven't for almost a decade. There is, of course, a very simple reason why I no longer have a credit card: I spent too much money when I did have one.

In fact, it is reckoned that people with credit cards spend an estimated 34 per cent more than those without them. It's just so easy to keep spending when you are buying with plastic! You can have what you want with the promise that you won't have to pay for it until the end of the month or even later. It sounds absolutely wonderful – too good to be true.

And, of course, it *is* too good to be true. Because what cripples you is the interest. And to make matters worse, you always end up buying something else with your credit card long before you've finished paying for the last thing, so you pay interest on that, too.

The average amount of debt per debtor in the UK

(excluding mortgages) is £10,000! Paying that much off is not easy. But imagine running up a bill so high that paying it off is not just difficult: it's downright impossible.

It is like this with God. He has pretty exacting standards about how our lives should be lived. Imagine that every failure to live his way added up against you, like interest on a credit card. Even if you walk six inches above the ground, talk with the animals and use the power from your halo to light a small town during the hours of darkness, you will soon run up a tab well beyond your ability to repay.

After all, even Mother Theresa doesn't claim to be all square with God.

Once upon a time . . .

Jesus once visited the house of a religious leader, a man who went to extreme lengths to make sure that he didn't sin. During dinner a prostitute broke in and began to wash Jesus' feet with her tears and dry them with her hair. The host showed disapproval. So Jesus did what came naturally: he told a story.

'There were two men,' he said, 'and both of them owed money to a money-lender. One owed the equivalent of fifty days' wages and the other the equivalent of five hundred days' wages. Neither could afford to repay their debt. So the money-lender cancelled both.

'Now: which one do you think was more grateful?'

'Why, the one with the bigger debt, I suppose,' replied the host. After all, the answer was obvious. 'Exactly,' said Jesus. It must have taken the religious leader a few moments to twig what was going on.

Jesus made it clear that whilst the prostitute owed God a greater debt than the religious leader did, neither of them could afford to pay, in spite of the leader's efforts. So God cancelled both debts.

It's the same with us. We run up debts with God that we can never hope to pay off. Knowing this, God has cancelled our debts. We do not deserve to have our debts cancelled; in fact, we deserve to meet the full consequences of our actions. But because he loves us, and for no other reason, God cancelled our debt. And he did this by becoming a human being and dying on the cross, in spite of his innocence.

It's a bit like someone coming along and paying off your credit card debt when you know you haven't got a chance of paying it yourself. By dying on the cross, that's exactly what Jesus did for us.

'A place called Hope'

On a recent trip to Thailand, I came across a place called Rainbow House. In Thai culture, disability is often frowned upon; in fact, a great many disabled and disfigured children are simply left by their parents on the steps of the government children's home. Their disabilities could range from severe mental or physical handicap to something as minor as a cleft lip. Because there are so many children and so few resources, they are left to vegetate, often three or four to a bed, without much human contact. I was told that those who were not mentally disabled when they came in soon became so as a result of the lack of attention, stimulation, love and warmth shown to them.

Rainbow House takes children from here and gives them hope. It is small, and can only cater for a few children at a time. But its aim is to salvage the least badly affected children. It seeks to love and care for them, to nurture them until they reach the point where they are capable of being adopted, sometimes by people outside Thailand. Rainbow House would long to give a new beginning to all the children dumped as 'substandard', but they find that their limited resources stretch only so far.

When I visited there, I was introduced to one little girl whose only flaw was that she was born without feet. Where her feet should have been were only stumps. She was highly intelligent, warm, kind, very pretty and full of life; yet she had been thrown away by her parents. After a spell in the government centre, she was rescued by the Rainbow House staff whilst she was still a baby. With shoes on, it was impossible to tell that she was not physically perfect. In fact, she could run faster than most people *with* feet. Without the help of

Rainbow House, she would almost certainly have died.

It is this kind of new beginning that God offers to us as a gift.

18

A twist in the tale

ALEXANDER the Great; Julius Caesar; Attilla the Hun; Henry VIII; Napoleon Bonaparte; Winston Churchill; Mohandis Gandhi; John F. Kennedy; Martin Luther King. What do all of these people have in common?

Well, they're all great men in one way or another. And they're all . . . well . . . dead!

But the extraordinary thing is that, although he was born over two thousand years ago, Christians claim that Jesus isn't dead. In fact, the whole of the Christian faith hangs around this point.

If you could conclusively prove that Jesus *hadn't* risen from the dead, then every church would have to close. You'd be the biggest thing to happen for two thousand years!

After all, Jesus is the most influential person ever to have lived. Our whole calendar system revolves around the year of his birth. Hundreds of thousands of books have been written about him. Millions of buildings are constructed in his honour. A quarter of the world's population claims to worship him. And his claim to this central position in history depends on his resurrection.

Who moved the stone?

A skilled lawyer called Frank Morrison took up this challenge. With a chip on his shoulder against Christianity, he set out to disprove the resurrection, but the more he looked into it, the more convinced he became that the alternatives to the resurrection just didn't add up.

Jesus died on the cross. He was taken down and placed in a tomb. The religious authorities got a military guard put on the tomb: they were afraid that there might be truth in the rumours that he would rise from the dead. They were afraid that the disciples would make it *appear* that he had risen from the dead by stealing the body. But when the women followers of Jesus visited the tomb three days later, they found no Roman Army detachment guarding the body.

In fact, they found no body. And the stone which had covered the tomb had been rolled away.

The Case of the Empty Tomb

So what are the options?

1. *Bodysnatching.* Now your first thought might be that the religious authorities had been right. In the dead of the

night, galvanised into concerted action, the disciples had put on their best camouflage, had picked up their swords, had taken their own lives into their hands and had stolen the body.

But is this really likely? On the day of Jesus' execution, the disciples had been scared for their lives. Peter had denied three times even *knowing* Jesus. In his account of events, the disciple John does not give a flattering picture of either himself or his fellow disciples. The Roman garrisons posted to Judea were often the bottom of the barrel, yet they were still more than a match for a bunch of scared, itinerant missionaries: especially since the price of failure was death!

The idea that the disciples were even co-ordinated enough to steal the body is a little far-fetched. But who else would have a motive to steal the body? Grave robbers? What interest would they have in a man whose only valuable possession – a robe – was forfeited to the state when he died, and who was so poor that he even had to be placed in a borrowed tomb! Besides, grave robbers before the age of Dr Frankenstein didn't steal bodies: they just stole the valuables.

What if the religious authorities stole the body themselves in order to stop the disciples from stealing it? Well in that case, why did they not simply produce the body after reports of the resurrection became widespread?

Perhaps, like something out of a Marx Brothers comedy, everybody got the wrong grave by mistake. Perhaps they left the dead Jesus in some other nearby tomb whilst they followed the trail of a *different* missing body. But is it really possible that in all the commotion, claims and counter-claims, it didn't occur to anyone to check the grave? Not even the Roman guard? Hardly! Producing the body must have been pretty high on the agendas of the religious leaders, who stood to lose their reputations; and of the Roman soldiers, who stood to lose their lives!

With no other candidates coming forward, the theft of the body seems a little unlikely.

2. *Surviving the Crucifixion.* But perhaps Jesus was not really dead after all. Perhaps the Roman soldiers goofed. What if making mincemeat of his back and then using it as a human wagon through hostile crowds didn't do the trick? What if being strapped to a wooden gallows and having a thick iron nail shattering each wrist left Jesus undaunted? Perhaps the blood loss, the increase with each breath of excruciating pain, and the spear lunged into his heart to ensure that he was dead, did not quite finish him off. And maybe, just maybe, he merely passed out on the cross, regained consciousness in the tomb, moved a very heavy stone singlehanded, defeated the soldiers without a weapon, and, careful not to leave any clues . . . escaped!

Then again, maybe not.

3. *Abduction by aliens.* It is probably fairly safe to assume that neither aliens nor Elvis swooped down to remove Jesus' lifeless corpse and take it away for a more dignified departure somewhere else. Just as it is probably fairly safe

to assume that Jesus was not an alien from Venus simply masquerading as a human being, who then beamed back up to his ship like something out of *Star Trek*.

'Elementary, my dear Watson'

Sir Arthur Conan Doyle's famous detective, the great Sherlock Holmes, used to say in an investigation that after you had eliminated the impossible, whatever you had left, however improbable, must be the truth. Given the weakness of the alternatives presented, therefore, the resurrection seems the most likely explanation for the missing body. In fact, it seems the *only* likely explanation for the missing body.

'And for my next trick . . .'

The New Testament writers, however, pay very little attention to the question of who removed the body: they do not use this as evidence for the resurrection at all. Instead, they rely on the testimony given by people who claimed to have seen Jesus after the time of his resurrection. The gospel writer Luke says that Jesus gave his sceptical disciples 'many convincing proofs that he was alive'. He appeared to the disciples themselves. He appeared to the entourage of women who followed him. And he appeared to a much wider group of people, as well.

Of course, no proof is absolute. Two thousand years later, we can't talk to the witnesses who saw Jesus after he had risen from the dead. We can't inspect the scene of the crime, take fingerprints or run tests. There is no mathematical formula which can prove that Jesus rose from the dead. You can't reduce it all down to

$$J+d/mc=2xyz^2$$

and hope that people are suitably impressed. However sensible the idea that Jesus rose from the dead may be, believing it to be true will still always ultimately be a matter of faith – not blind faith. Faith based on evidence, but faith all the same.

But then, we take things on faith every day of our lives. I have faith that the chair I am sitting on to write this will hold me up. If I catch a train, I have faith that it will go to the advertised place and not the other end of the country. If I get on a bus, I have faith that the driver has passed his test and is not going to crash. I have faith that no one has maliciously poisoned my lunch.

In fact, we take literally hundreds of steps of faith every single day. And all of the most important things in our lives are a matter of faith. I have faith that my wife loves me. My children have faith that I love them. Not blind faith. Faith based on evidence. But faith, all the same.

Ultimately it was the *belief* of the early disciples that they had seen the resurrected Jesus of Nazareth, *their faith*, which led to the spread of Christianity throughout the ancient Roman world. Thousands and thousands of lives were changed. What's more, Christians were so convinced by their experiences, and by the stories of the resurrection, that they were prepared to die rather than give up this faith. And they often did.

It didn't end there. Down through the centuries, millions of perfectly rational and intelligent human beings have reached the conclusion that the resurrection is true. They come from every tribe and nation in the world. And they have been willing to give their lives for it.

Part Four

The Choice

19
What is a Christian, anyway?

THE TERM 'Christian' simply means 'little Christ'. It was probably used initially as a term of abuse. However, it stuck, and it is now the most widely used name for Jesus' followers.

A Christian, then, is a person who follows Jesus. But following Jesus is much more than simply a case of believing in God and the Bible. Jesus did not ask his first disciples on the shores of Lake Galilee, 'Believe in God.' He said, '*Follow me.*'

When asked in surveys, the vast majority of people in this country say that they believe in God. But it's easy then to make the mistake of thinking that this is exactly the same as being a Christian. When you think about it, that's ridiculous, because even Jesus' enemies believed in God!

Lots of people follow parts of Jesus' teaching, but this does not by itself make them Christians. Of course, Christians *do* follow Jesus' teaching; but there's a lot more to being a Christian than that.

Nor is a follower of Jesus someone who merely goes to

church. Jesus spent most of his time with prostitutes and criminals, but he never told them to 'Put on your best gear and come on down to the synagogue with me. That should do the trick.' He said, *'Follow me.'*

Although Christians *do* go to church, we all know that there are a great many people who go religiously but who are *not* actually Christians. After all, going to church no more makes you a Christian than going to Wembley makes you a footballer!

Nor are Christians merely those born into a 'Christian country' or a 'Christian family'. Christianity is not an official status, and it's not something that can be caught like a virus by standing too close to someone else who is infected. Jesus did not say to the foreigners, immigrants and exiles he encountered, 'Apply for your Jewish passport. It's your ticket to heaven.' He said *'Follow me.'*

'Just like starting over'

So what *does* it mean to follow Jesus? What *is* a Christian?

Well, you can't really be a Marxist or a Thatcherite unless you follow properly the teachings of Karl Marx or Margaret Thatcher, and try to put into practice the principles of what they have taught. In the same way, you can't really be a Christian without building your life around the principles that Jesus taught. You can always call yourself a Marxist. But unless you actually understand the principles that Marx taught and base your life on them, you're simply deluding yourself. The label you've given yourself is meaningless.

Of course, lots of people say that they follow the teachings of Jesus. But when you ask them what this entails, they say, 'Well, it's something about loving your neighbour and turning the other cheek, isn't it?' Jesus did teach about loving your neighbour and turning the other cheek, but anything more than a quick glance at his teaching shows that there's much more to it than that. In fact, the heart of Jesus' message is how we go about restoring our severed relationship with God and the broken relationships we have with one another.

It's really about the chance to start over. To begin again.

20

Is there life before death?

THE GENERAL opinion is that Christianity is really concerned with what happens to people when they die. It's about whether you go on to 'heaven' or 'hell' for the rest of eternity. But in fact, the New Testament talks very little about an afterlife. This does not mean that the writers of the New Testament didn't believe in an afterlife; it just means that it wasn't very high on their list of priorities.

The Case of the Phantom Bus Driver

I first started going to church when I was 14 to impress a girl called Mary Hooper. She went to the local church youth group, and I fancied her; so I went along, and stayed. It seemed like every other week someone would be invited to do a talk about their hobby or what they did for a living. It didn't matter if it was chartered accounting or lepidopterology (which sounded rude until I discovered that it was only the study of butterflies). They used to bore us silly for about twenty minutes. And then, without fail, whatever the subject they had just talked about, they'd all end the same way. In fact, they seemed to use almost exactly the same words.

'If you're not a Christian,' they used to say, 'and you walk out of here and get run over by a Number 68 bus, where will you be then?' The answer seemed all too obvious. I'd be spinning round under the back wheels! But at a deeper level, the question posed a number of problems for me. You see, I didn't live on a bus route. And the walk from the church to my house passed no major roads and no bus stops. And anyway, how would the driver know that I wasn't a Christian?

In my mind's eye I saw a phantom bus driver careering out of control down the side streets of Croydon. He was foaming at the mouth and wearing a crazed expression on his face. Perched on his nose were specially adapted X-ray specs capable of telling apart those who were Christians from those who weren't. He was grinning moronically and with evil pleasure at the thought of running down a certain S. Chalke of South Norwood.

This didn't make me decide to become a Christian, of course! But it did make me very aware of the Green Cross Code, and slightly wary of buses!

The booking office is now open

It's a common misconception that the sole purpose of

being a Christian is to book your seat for heaven. Pie in the sky when you die. But although it's good to be reminded sometimes that Christians *are* going to have eternal life, we have to put this in context.

All too often, Christianity seems like an eternal life assurance policy. The French mathematician Blaise Pascal, for instance, reckoned that you couldn't possibly *know* whether or not God existed. But it was terribly important for people to make a decision. So, he said, it was best to be on the safe side. It was best to believe in the existence of God. That way, if God did exist, you'd ensured favour in the next life. And if he didn't exist, what had you lost by believing that he did? In Pascal's thinking, it was best to hedge your bets.

But this misses the point entirely. The question is not, 'If you were to die tonight, where would you be then?' The real question is, 'If you *don't* die tonight, where will you be tomorrow morning?'

Becoming a Christian is about the next five, ten or fifty years. It's just as much about the time *before* your death as it is about what happens to you *after* your death. After all, if Christianity were just about where you spent the after-life, then the real aim for everyone would be to delay becoming a Christian as long as possible. That way you could live as wild and immoral a life as possible and make up for everything in a final, dramatic deathbed conversion. The trick would be to know when to take this big step. You would gamble on being close enough to have your cake and still be able to eat it.

Body and soul

There's an old hymn which dates from the American Civil War, which goes:

> John Brown's body lies a-moulding in the grave,
> But his soul goes marching on!

It reflects the opinion of a great many people that human beings are made up of two components – body and soul – which separate after death. The body rots in the grave, but the soul goes on to the afterlife, like Patrick Swayze in the film *Ghost*.

It's as though people go through their lives like Thunderbird 2 (the big green one with the removable pod). Then, when they die, they jettison this outer hull and proceed on to the next life in Thunderbird 4 (the little yellow submarine kept within the belly of Thunderbird 2). Thunderbird 2 is the body, Thunderbird 4 the soul.

Actually, this view owes more to the ancient Greek philosophers than it does to the Bible. The Bible says that God is concerned with the *whole* of your life. This doesn't just begin with your death. Jesus said, 'I've come to give you life at its best.' His teaching is a mine of great advice about everyday life in the here-and-now.

The score at half time

I remember talking with a friend once at a party. I asked him what he wanted to do with the rest of his life. 'I don't know,' he said. Whatever I suggested, he just kept saying, 'I don't know.' Eventually, I asked him what he considered to be the point of his life. 'I don't know,' he said again. 'Life is so meaningless. I feel like I'm playing in a football match. It's half time, and I've come in for the oranges. I'm not even sure whether I want to go back out to play the second half, let alone which way I should kick if I do.'

Jesus' teaching is about how to play, and how to want to play, the second half. It's not just about what you do when the match is over.

The real thing

The life Jesus came to offer people is a life of a better quality much more than it is a life of a bigger quantity. Last year I went to Madame Tussauds. I was impressed with how real some of the wax figures looked, yet I could still tell the difference between them and the numerous tourists who were trying very hard to stand absolutely still and be mistaken for a waxwork.

The difference between the 'best' *life* that Jesus comes to offer, and the meaningless *existence* of my friend at the party, is the difference between the waxworks at Madame

Tussauds and real people. Or the difference between a postcard of a place and the place itself. Until I actually went to New York, my only knowledge of it was through films and photographs. I'd seen so many by that time that I thought I had a pretty good idea of what to expect. But in fact, it was completely different. Postcards capture the view, but they can never capture the atmosphere. They can never become real.

It's the same thing with life. Unless you're tapped in to what God says about it, the best you can experience is like a postcard. Jesus insisted that there's a quality of life you can only discover by following him.

That's why making a decision about Jesus Christ is so important. And it won't just affect you. It will also affect those around you. Because real life is not only about what you can *get* out of it; it's also about what you can *put into* it.

21

At home with the dunderheads

IT MIGHT seem strange to think that Jesus would pick such an odd assortment of people to become his closest friends and followers. He seems to have offered this real life to a bunch of dunderheads.

They were predominantly rural fishermen, with a tax collector and a revolutionary thrown in for good measure. They had no formal religious training – the only kind of education available at the time. But then, neither did Jesus. They were none of them priests, or anything to do with the official religious hierarchy. But then, neither was Jesus.

Why didn't he choose the first-century equivalent of university graduates?

Ordinary people

John recounts that Jesus' disciples were ordinary people who constantly got the wrong end of the stick. Jesus spent a great deal of time, energy and patience getting them to the place where the penny finally dropped even about who he really was. They suffered from chronic foot-in-mouth disease. They were ill-prepared for the arrest and trial of Jesus. Just when he needed their support the most, that's when they deserted him.

Jesus aimed his message at ordinary people. He talked to ordinary people. He healed and challenged ordinary people. He himself came from the stock of ordinary people. So it makes sense that his followers should have been, for the most part, ordinary people.

The disciples fill most of us with confidence, because most of us are ordinary people too. Like the disciples, all of us make mistakes. Like the disciples, most of us often get the wrong end of the stick. Yet, like the disciples, God can use us to do extraordinary things. And like the disciples, God offers us real life.

You don't have to be special to accept this offer. You don't need to be clever. You don't need to be beautiful. You don't need qualifications, or a job. You don't need to be married, or single. You don't need to be charming, or good. You just have to be alive – and willing. The choice is yours.

What Next?

22

Becoming a Christian

IN ONE sense, it's easy to become a Christian, in spite of the fact that it is a big step and a serious commitment. It's simply a case of shifting the focus of your life from you onto God and deciding to live your life God's way.

But be warned: becoming a Christian may make things difficult for you. If it's an *easy* life you're after, then whatever you do, *don't* become a Christian. But if you want a rewarding life, packed with meaning, then don't pass up on the chance. If you want to change the world for the better, this is the best way to do it.

Like most good relationships, becoming a follower of Jesus starts with a conversation. So all you need to do is pray, which is just talking to God. You don't need any special language; you don't even need to speak out loud, although this might help.

Just tell God, in your own words, that you have decided to live life his way. That you are serious about this commitment. That you are sorry for having ignored his way in the past. And that you are now open to the guidance of his Holy Spirit.

Your life as a Christian has begun!

23

The Good Church Guide

ONE OF the biggest and most widespread errors in the English language concerns the word 'Church'. People have the wrong idea about it all. It conjures up images of a big old building. It's freezing inside, with dry rot and a belltower.

Actually, 'Church' is a collective noun. We know about collective nouns: one sheep is a sheep, but a whole gang of sheep is called a 'flock'. One cow is a cow, but a whole bunch of cows is a 'herd'. One goose is a goose, but a whole band of marauding geese is called a 'gaggle'. So it is with 'Church'. One Christian is a Christian, but a number of Christians gathered together is called a 'Church'.

So if you get stopped in the street and asked for directions to the nearest church, the answer is not, 'Down the street, turn left and it's just next to the pub.' Because the Church is Jesus' followers, and it is wherever they happen to be. It is the collective noun for Christians meeting together on Sunday and the rest of the week to learn more about living life God's way.

What this means, of course, is that a church is only as boring or exciting as the people in it. So if the idea of church fills you with dread, and you break out in a sudden and uncontrollable fit of yawns, it means that you've been looking at the wrong church. Or that you've been looking at things too much from the outside.

The world-famous solo double act

It is difficult and frequently demoralising to do things alone. We lack the help and support we so often need to get the job done. After all, even the Lone Ranger had Tonto. Laurel had Hardy. French had Saunders. Ron had Nancy. Marks had Spencer. Tom had Jerry. Thelma had Louise. Throughout history, people have found that working alone is daunting. It's also very ineffective: it is easier to work in teams.

But there is more to Church than this. Church provides an environment for Christians to share with other Christians. They can share their experiences and their beliefs. They can share their doubts. They can share their joys and their woes, their prayers and their concerns. And Church also provides an opportunity for Christians to worship together and to learn more about God together.

All I wanted was a beer

But there seem to be so many different kinds of church on offer: Anglican, Catholic, Baptist, Methodist, Pentecostal, Salvation Army . . . the list appears endless. Which one's the *real* thing?

Well, they all are.

Just the other week, I was in New York on business. I sat in an hotel bar with a friend and we ordered a couple of beers. We should have know that this was a bad move in the land of ultimate choice.

'What d'ya want?' asked the waiter. 'We got: Bass Ale; Becks; Budweiser; Carling; Coors; Corona; Fosters; Heineken; Killian's; Labatts; Löwenbrau; Michelob; Miller Genuine Draft; Old Milwaukee; Sam Adams; Sol . . .'

The list seemed to go on for ever. Eventually we chose the first one we'd heard of, and we breathed a sigh of relief that the trauma of making decisions was over. Little did we know!

'D'ya want that canned, bottled or draught? Low alcohol or high alcohol? Tall glass or short glass? Ice or no ice? And how would you like to pay? We take cash, American Express, Diner's Card, Visa, Barclaycard . . .' The list went on. Eventually, we placed an order.

Two minutes later, he came back. 'I'm sorry, gentlemen, but we're out of that. You'll have to order again.'

There are seemingly infinite variations of the same thing to cater for slight differences in taste, style and preference.

They might be different labels with slightly different flavours, but ultimately they're all beer.

Horses for courses

It's the same with denominations: they're all basically the same thing. Because Church is a collective noun, church denominations differ only as much as the Christians who make them up. Some people like modern music and some like traditional music. Some people like formal clothes, whilst others prefer a more casual approach. (Some churches like their ministers to wear dresses, though only if they're men!) Some people like the language to be 𝔳𝔢 𝔬𝔩𝔡𝔢 𝔴𝔬𝔯𝔩𝔡𝔢, whilst others prefer a more contemporary approach. Some are quiet and meditative, others more loud and raucous. The truth is, they're all just the same thing with different wrappers. They're all Church, because they're all Christians meeting together to live life God's way.

You may not find the first church you try quite to your taste. Don't be put off: keep looking. If you already know people who are Christians, ask their advice.

24

Reading the Bible

As a Christian, you will need a copy of the Bible, God's instruction book. Trying to manage as a Christian without the Bible is as daft as buying a brand-new car but refusing even to look at the manual.

But let's be honest. Most Bibles are not exactly the best adverts you've ever seen for the Christian faith. I mean, thick black leatherbound books with gold writing down their spines saying 𝕳𝖔𝖑𝖞 𝕭𝖎𝖇𝖑𝖊 are not going to compete too well in the bookshops with the latest John Grisham, Jilly Cooper or Danielle Steele.

It's not that there's anything wrong with the Bible. In fact, it's without doubt the most profound and life-changing book ever written. It's not even that the Bible lacks excitement. There's enough sex, violence and bad language in it to rival anything at the box office. And of course, the Bible is still the world's number one bestseller. Most of us have at some point been given one.

The problem is that sales do not equal readership. Most of us use Bibles to press flowers. Otherwise they just stand on the shelf collecting dust. Part of the problem is the title and the cover design: they put you off even before you get to page one.

'Only the names have been changed'

So what title would give the Bible that essential quality to make people pull a copy off the shelves in eager anticipation? What could you call the Bible that would make people desperate to read it? What would stop people being ashamed to read it on the train or in the bus? After all, it's got all the right ingredients. People would read it if only they knew. So what title could possibly reflect these ingredients?

Well, I think I've come up with a reasonable alternative. For a long time I've thought that a much better title for the Bible would be . . . *Against All Odds*! It packs both excitement and punch. But there are three more reasons why I think that *Against All Odds* would be a good title for the Bible:

- *Against All Odds*, God forgives our rebellion and outright rejection of him and the life that he offers us. Why did God not simply declare Planet Earth a mistake? Why didn't he just scrap it and start again with a new project somewhere else? And why did God go to the ultimate lengths of forgiveness by becoming a human being himself? It runs completely against the odds.

- If that's all there was to it, it would be reason enough why *Against All Odds* is a great title. And life would be a fantastic deal about which none of us could complain. But there's more. God's forgiveness is only half the story, because *Against All Odds* God has also chosen to work with us as partners. The Bible is a catalogue of all sorts of ordinary men and women through whom God chose to do extraordinary things because they were willing to trust him and give their lives to him.

- What is more, *Against All Odds* the Bible is the story of how God provides the resources for people to live their lives his way. Christians always talk about God the Father, God the Son and God the Holy Spirit. We've discussed God the Father and Jesus – God the Son. But so far we've not really mentioned God the Holy Spirit. Basically, it's the Holy Spirit's job to help us live life God's way. The Holy Spirit helps us to be the kind of person God wants us to be, and the kind of person *we* want to be. The Holy Spirit is the power pack for equipping Christians in their everyday lives. Without the Holy Spirit, we would be as pathetic as a modern army going into battle armed only with peashooters. The Bible is filled with stories of the ways in which the Holy Spirit did equip and continues to equip people to live the life God offers.

To begin at the end

The Bible was originally written in ancient Greek and Hebrew, so unless you are fluent in these languages, you will need a translation. There are a number of translations available, although the differences between them are very small indeed. The most important thing is to find one whose language you can understand. If you know people who are Christians, they should be able to help you choose.

Unlike most books, it's probably best *not* to start at the beginning. Instead, start with one of the gospels, the bits of the Bible that tell the story of Jesus. Start perhaps with the books of Mark or Luke. These are found in the New Testament, toward the back of the Bible.

It is important to think about what you read: quality is more important than quantity. It takes most Christians several years to read through the whole Bible from cover to cover, so don't be put off by its length or complexity.

25

Praying

THERE is an old Burt Reynolds film in which he finds himself out at sea. Literally. Convinced that he will not make the swim back to the shore, he does something he has not done for thirty years: he prays. 'Oh God,' he says, when he is still some way out, 'I swear, if you get me out of this alive, I'll give you everything I have!'

As he gets nearer the shore, he modifies his position. 'Oh God,' he prays, 'if you get me out of this alive, I'll give you half of everything I have!' Gradually, as he nears land, his need lessens. And so does his offer until, finally ashore and alive, he has 'bargained' God down to nothing.

Only in times of crisis

Christianity is, above all, a relationship with God and his Son, Jesus Christ. And as any good marriage guidance counsellor will tell you, relationships depend for their survival on communication. Prayer is basically communication between people and God: it is a way of talking to and hearing from God. So it's stupid to leave it just for times of crisis.

It's stupid, for one thing, to ignore good advice and companionship when it's freely offered. But it's also very rude only to talk to God when you want something. This turns a relationship into a business arrangement, and that is not what Christianity is all about. So keep praying, because however hard it may seem at times, it's the lifeline of the Christian faith.

26

The adventure continues

AN ENGLISH businessman sat on a train, almost alone in his compartment. As the train pulled out of a station, two young American men came in and sat opposite him. They talked quietly to each other. The businessman, who had been looking at the scenery and enjoying the sun, sought to regain his privacy by reading his newspaper.

Suddenly, and without warning, one of the Americans began to shake and slipped off his seat. His companion seemed completely unfazed by this epileptic fit. He loosened his friend's clothing and made him comfortable. From the way he moved, it was obvious that he had done this many times before. He looked up and saw that the businessman was alarmed.

'Don't worry. This happens a lot. He'll be all right in a bit.'

'Is there anything I can do?' asked the businessman.

'No. He'll be fine. We just have to wait a bit.'

As they talked, the American revealed that he travelled everywhere with his friend, just to make sure that he was all right. In fact, he had given up his job a few years before to do exactly that. The businessman was deeply impressed by this dedication and self-sacrifice, and said so.

'You don't understand,' the American replied. 'We fought together in Vietnam, and he saved my life. I would not be alive today if it weren't for him. So you see, I owe everything to this man. Everything I have, everything I am and everything I will be is not enough to say thank you.'

If Jesus went to the extreme lengths of dying on a cross in order to give us real life, then we owe him everything. Everything we have, everything we are and everything we will ever be.

That's why I became a Christian in the first place. It's why I remain a Christian some twenty-five years later. And it's why I'll still be a Christian in another twenty-five years' time.

27

Finding out more

Two books which cover the same sort of ground as this one:

- J. John, *Dead Sure*. IVP Frameworks, 1989. A fresh look at the arguments *for* the Christian faith in a new and colourful format.
- Stephen Gaukroger, *It Makes Sense*. Scripture Union, 1987. A very readable examination of the most common arguments *against* the Christian faith.

Two books which take the arguments further:

- C. S. Lewis, *Mere Christianity*. Fontana, 1955. An intelligent look at the basics of the Christian faith, available in most bookshops.
- R. T. France, *The Evidence for Jesus*. Hodder and Stoughton, 1986. A detailed look at the existence and teaching of Jesus.

Two books for those who have just become Christians:

- Michael Green, *New Life, New Lifestyle*. Hodder and Stoughton, 1973.
- Nicky Gumbel, *A Life Worth Living*. Kingsway, 1994.